Something I've Never Felt Before

Something I've Never Felt Before

How teenagers cope with grief

Doris Zagdanski

HILL OF CONTENT

First published in Australia 1990
by Hill of Content Publishing
86 Bourke Street, Melbourne, Australia

Reprinted 1992, 1994

Designed by Graphic Divine
Front Cover by Sarn Potter
Typeset in Australia by Midland Typesetters, Maryborough, Vic.
Printed in Australia by Australian Print Group, Maryborough, Vic.

National Library of Australia
Cataloguing-in-Publication data

Zagdanski, Doris, 1954–
How Teenagers cope with grief: something I've never felt before.

ISBN 0 85572 199 5.

1. Bereavement in adolescence. 2. Grief–Psychological aspects. 3. Adolescent psychology. I. Title.

155.937088055

For my daughters, Kate and Kristen.

You help me to remember that there is still meaning in life even though we live without one who meant so much.

CONTENTS

ACKNOWLEDGEMENTS

Even at a glance it is clear that this book is more than a singular effort. So many people contributed throughout the process of consulting, interviewing, writing and rewriting. It's now my turn to say thanks.

I think firstly of the core group of young people whose words, spoken with courage and honesty, have illustrated my thoughts:

Vesna Angelevska
Katrina Bloot-Hoofd
Joanne Cameron
Katherine Cameron
James Collings
Robert Collings
Adam Collins
Haley Good
Troy Griggs
Joylene Nicholson
Kate Renzenbrink
Janet Roberts
Lloyd Roberts
Donna Rutherford
Kirsty Storvik
Mandy Storvik
Anna Theleritis
Jenny Theleritis
Adrian Viccars
Rachelle Westlake
Andrew Zagdanski

Next I acknowledge the professional support, guidance and evaluation of Freda Wright, Pupil Welfare Co-ordinator, and Peter Schmidt, Principal, both of Matthew Flinders Girls' High School, Geelong; Irene Renzenbrink, Social

Worker, John Allison/Monkhouse; Bob Coffey, teacher and friend; Penny Bloot-Hoofd, nursing sister, friend and sounding-board. Special thanks to Tobin Brothers Funeral Directors, namely Des Tobin for giving me access to the resources of Death and Bereavement Educational Services, and his staff, Allan Anderson and Kay Sudborough, who assisted so enthusiastically with the manuscript preparation. Also, Valerie Gilpin, Bayside School Support Centre, Victorian Ministry of Education, whose lecture inspired the school recovery policy information.

It is also important that I recognize the impact and influence of the hundreds of school students and families whom I have met in my work as a funeral director and bereavement educator. I am sure that a small part of you is contained within the larger whole which has become this book. Then there are the special families of Jenny Ryan, Amber Stahl and Tristan Murrihy who, amidst their own grief, have given permission to include their stories so that others may learn.

And finally, at home, Peter - my husband, friend and manuscript typist - and daughters, Kate and Kristen, have endured my hours of seclusion being forever patient and always accepting.

Introduction

Many teenagers grieve silently.

I was again convinced of this today after speaking to a Year 10 class at a local secondary school. As I was leaving, a shy-looking youth asked if he could speak with me. He told me of his fishing mate who had died a few years ago and of the story he had written about him in his school journal. 'But no one has ever read it,' he said. 'I keep it in my locker. But you can read it if you like.'

After that I went home to write the final words of this book, convinced that kids need this information. No, we all need it.

Shakespeare was right when one of his characters said, 'Give sorrow words.' But there is nothing fictitious about the words in this book. The kids are real, their stories are real, and their hurt is real. All they ask of us is to listen to them, not just with our ears, but with our hearts.

Having said this, the initial concept for this book actually came from a conversation with some school teachers in which we discussed the plight of teenagers who were trying to cope with death and grief - especially for the first time. The suggestion was made that I should have a go at writing something to help these kids. And so the idea was born.

However, in truth, I believe the real seed was sown some years ago when my own daughter died. Her death meant, amongst other things, that I began a search for understanding. I did not understand why my family had been singled out for such a tragedy - or so it seemed at the time. Moreover, I did not understand myself any more - my reactions, my needs, my moods, my pain.

I was scared. Life had not prepared me for this; they didn't teach me about death at school. In fact, I quickly realized that death was a subject that no one really wanted to talk about.

Here I was, a grown woman with a university education, but when it came to the crunch all the knowledge in my head was no help at all to fix what was happening in my heart. I decided I had to find out about this thing called *grief*. I knew I had some more learning to do but this time I wasn't just going to fill my head with facts. I was going to fill the empty space inside with something useful to help me cope with life - as it really is.

And this is what I learnt. I discovered that even smart people can't beat grief. Trying to pretend that you were all right didn't work. Oh yes, on the outside you could fool people, but on the inside the hurt just muddled around in your stomach, in your throat, in your heart and in your head – until you thought you were going crazy.

I also learnt that crying was okay. It didn't mean that I was weak or feeling sorry for myself. Tears simply mean that when tension builds up inside you, whatever the cause, you can release some of it by 'having a good cry'.

I learnt that I couldn't make it alone. I needed to ask for help. That wasn't easy for me. I sought out support groups, especially people who would listen. I talked out my feelings. I read about the feelings of others who had also felt loss. It all helped.

Above all, I came to accept that life doesn't always turn out the way we expect. Good and bad, happy and sad things happen to us all. We mightn't like it, but that's the way the world works and we don't get much say in it.

We do, however, get to choose whether we will hate the world forever, or whether we will try our best to live with the events, opportunities and people that come our way in life. It took me a long time to realize that, but it's been an important lesson to learn.

Doris Zagdanski

PART I

UNDER-STANDING GRIEF

CHAPTER 1

About grief

For days on end I would think about all the things we did together.

Grief is the word used to describe the feelings and reactions we have when something devastating happens in our lives. We often associate grief only with death. However, we can actually grieve as a result of losing anything we value or anyone for whom we care deeply.

This is how one 19-year-old described the break-up between himself and his girlfriend:

> *The night it all came to an end and the weeks that followed were to become the hardest period of my life. A part of me died.*
>
> *For the past two years I devoted everything to this one person whom I absolutely adored and loved very much. 'This is not happening,' I said to myself, but it was. What am I going to do, how am I going to cope with her gone . . .*
>
> *For days on end I would think of all the things we did together, and would just break down into uncontrollable fits of crying. I found it very hard to sleep at night and motivate myself to do things. I was just not interested.*
>
> *Depression soon set in and thoughts of ending my existence were becoming a reality. But that was not the answer, how could I be so selfish. I couldn't do that to the people I love and of course to myself . . .*
>
> *Two months have gone by since we parted ways, and still I find it difficult to comprehend*

why it happened the way it did. I miss her dearly. I would give anything to have her back. I still love her very much and our memories I will treasure for the rest of my life. She was so damned special and I blew it. I'll never forgive myself for it either. I want her back!

The hurts and disillusioned feelings of grief can also come from shattered hopes and dreams, lost security and unfulfilled expectations.

My best friend at school is Rebecca. Well . . . I like her but she doesn't really like me. You see, it's because I'm fat. Kid's don't like fat people. So I don't have many friends.

Two brothers described their reactions to their parents' separation saying:

The shock – it hit right in the guts. 'Is this really happening?' I thought. I knew these things happened but not to me.

I felt cheesed off with him for not being a good Dad and at what he did to Mum . . . I could have punched him and put him into hospital.

Many people remember the death of a pet as their first real experience of loss and grief.

I found it hard to take it knowing that I had waited 11 months for the foal to be born and then to find it dead . . . I knew then I could never get her in foal again. Even though I want to I can't handle the thought of it dying again.

My first experience with death was when a dog died when I was young. It was upsetting and it took a while to get over but I understood what had happened. Since then I have lost many pets and my grandmothers and one grandfather. I never knew those grandparents well, and the death of my pets was probably more upsetting to me than that of my grandparents.

It is said, that regardless of the reason for our grief, there can be similarities in the way we respond. Grief is okay for anyone who is hurting. Boys and girls, men and women all need to grieve. Even though it can be scary - something you've never felt before - it is still a normal way to behave.

The good news is that inside most of us there is a great deal of untouched strength and creativity. When we are facing a crisis we need to reach deep down inside and use what's already there to help us through the tough times. This book will give you some hints on how to do this. Hopefully then you will be able to face each new day knowing that the knot in your stomach will not be there forever.

> *It's a mixture of being alone and cold and lost. It's a heavy feeling - you're tired, no energy, you just drag yourself along. It's a feeling of your stomach being in your toes . . . I never want to feel like that again. It was so off.*
>
> Janet, aged 15,
> after her schoolfriend died.

> *I've been thinking about it. It's starting to make sense. It's become clearer. I'm more at ease with my feelings, I can understand them better.*
>
> Janet, 12 months later

CHAPTER 2

Thoughts and feelings. Are they normal?

Sometimes when I'm in town and I see friends walking around with their Mums I think: 'What about me? Why haven't I got a Mum?'

Have you ever watched peas cooking in a saucepan? When they're first dropped into the boiling water they just sink to the bottom. They don't move. They just sit there as if they're a bit stunned.

Then the heat gets them moving and they bounce around almost in a frenzy. They bump, crash, thump and spin around. Blindly. Aimlessly.

When the heat is turned down the commotion subsides. Slowly, gently, they cease their agitation. They float, they steady and begin to settle.

Grief can make us behave a bit like those frenzied peas. We're given the bad news and suddenly we've got all these feelings buzzing around inside us. We may not know what to do, where to turn or how to react!

Haley, aged 15, described it like this when her boyfriend was killed in a car accident:

> *I felt lost, lonely, no one to turn to, confused. I felt as though my heart had been stolen and would never be found. I felt like I was being torn apart and could never be put back together. I felt as though the world and my life were falling apart and it wasn't worth living the heartache.*

When Joanne, aged 14, was told of her grandmother's death she recalled:

> *I was shocked, devastated, couldn't believe she'd died, confused, numb and angry.*

After being told of her best friend and next-door neighbour's death, Anna, aged 15, reacted like this:

> *At first I couldn't comprehend what the tragic news really was and I broke out into tears. I was not even listening to what my Mum had actually said . . . I was totally shocked, uncontrollable tears, angry and scared.*

The following pages describe common feelings which we may expect when we are grieving. While some reactions might surprise us or even seem a bit strange or scary, be assured that they're all quite normal.

These reactions can be very changeable. Some days won't be so bad but then others just seem impossible. It's often a case of taking three steps forward and two steps back. It's hard work to keep moving forward but it can be done.

Try to remember that while these feelings can be very intense in the early days, weeks and months after a death, they slowly lessen as we learn to accept what has happened and adapt to the changes that this loss will make in our life.

The most common reaction to hearing some unexpected or bad news is a complete sense of shock and disbelief. Luckily our body automatically protects us from this shock and special hormones are pumped into our system. They can create a feeling like numbness.

Sometimes we might not want to believe the news and we try to pretend that it's all a dream. We may even continue to act as if nothing has happened. For many people it takes quite a while for the truth to really sink in.

> *I thought I would have cried when I was first told but I think I just couldn't believe she had died . . . it took quite a while before it really sunk in.*

> *I didn't know whether to believe the news. Maybe it wasn't all happening, maybe it was all a horrible dream.*

> *I was shocked. I thought she's gotta be alive, gotta be in hospital and be O.K. It couldn't get through to me that she wasn't alive no more.*

> *I'd never had to face this sort of news and I knew I wasn't ready for it either. It was too sudden. It was just impossible.*

As we begin to fully realize what's happened we start to react in different ways. We also see people around us reacting – often very differently from us.

> *My mum told me the news and I didn't cry. My sisters did but I wasn't really that close to her.*

Remember that no reaction is really right or wrong. Because we're all individuals, our reactions will reflect our own personality, our relationship with the person who died and our own special way of coping with stress. Grief is stress. Grief hurts. And it makes us wonder why it's happened to us.

> *Often I asked myself, 'Why did she have to die?' and still no one has an answer for me.*

> *It was hard to believe. But the one thing was why Mum? . . . Mostly I just asked myself and God WHY did it happen. WHY?*

We also begin to realize that death means the loss of many opportunities - so many things we'd planned to do that just can't be done any more. This realization can make us sad.

> *It just got to you -*
> *no more Jenny*
> *no more going out with her*
> *no more getting into trouble*
> *no more mischief*
> *no more climbing in my bedroom window*

> *It's not until you're deprived of something that you realize how much that something meant to you.*

Thoughts like this can make the world seem unjust and life unfair.

Why did it have to be her? Why couldn't it be me? She only had a life of 15 years.

Why did she die when she wasn't sick or anything?

Then, as we look at the people around us going about their usual business, we may even envy their happiness and seemingly carefree lives.

Sometimes when I'm in town and I see friends walking around with their Mums I think 'What about me? Why haven't I got a Mum?'

I try to avoid them (girls with their boyfriends) . . . they look so happy. It just hurts to see them together.

We may have angry thoughts directed at the world and the people in it:
for causing the death
for not being able to cure the illness
for dying and leaving us
for not understanding our feelings
for making thoughtless remarks
and for going on with life as though nothing has happened.

I felt angry at God for taking her away. She was the only Nana I had. All of my grandparents are dead.

I was angry because he didn't live longer than 60.

I really hate it when my friends say, 'I wish my Mum was dead.' One time, my friend was saying things about her mother and I said, 'Just consider yourself lucky that you've got a mother.'

We can also be angry with ourselves. Perhaps we wish we hadn't had that last argument. We may now regret what was said and feel guilty about it.

I wish I wasn't mad at you on Monday.

We may also regret things that we failed to do or say and now it seems too late.

After they were killed I felt so guilty. I kept blaming myself for what happened. I thought that if I'd been home they would have spent the day with me at my house instead of travelling back home that night.

. . . and I wish she hadn't gone so that I could say sorry and all that . . .

I remembered a dream I had a couple of weeks beforehand. It was exactly the same as how the accident happened. I kept blaming myself for her death because if I could have remembered the dream I would have been able to stop what happened by warning someone.

When death is due to suicide, in the thoughts of survivors, there can be heightened regret, guilt and shame as well. Searching for reasons and placing blame can also become a natural preoccupation linked to the need to know and ask 'why?'

Even though we might really miss the person who has died, it's possible to feel some relief for them too. This is especially true if their death followed a prolonged illness or period of unhappiness in their lives.

At times I wish she was here but other times I'm glad she's gone because she's happy and peaceful.

Today is just over one month since Grandpa died. I feel sad, yet glad, that he didn't have to suffer . . .

In a way I am glad that she died because my mother was in really bad pain for more than 11 years.

Where do all these feelings lead?

CHAPTER 3

Effects and behaviours. Are they normal too?

When I'm walking around the place I'll hear his voice and turn around and see him standing behind me.

Grief also affects our behaviour, our sleep, our appetite, and our concentration among other things. Very soon we realize that it seems to affect everything we think and do.

> *I usually think about her at least once a day and often it's the last thought that goes through my mind before I go to sleep.*

When our minds are working overtime, it can be hard to relax and switch off our thoughts - especially when we're alone or lying in bed at night.

> *My Mum reckons I was screaming in my dream NO! NOT JENNY. NOT HER!*

> *I have always had dreams of my Mum trying to kill me but I have never had a good dream about her.*

When our thoughts are so preoccupied with the person who has died, we can easily imagine seeing them or hearing their voice.

> *I'll walk past my bedroom and see him sitting on my bed or when I'm walking around the place I'll hear his voice and turn around and see him standing behind me.*

> *When I go into her house I hear her voice like she's calling for me.*

Dreams, thoughts and reactions like these can make us feel afraid or panicky.

I'd never felt it before and it scared me. I didn't like it.

I wanted to be around people . . . not alone . . . some of the anger is gone but I'm still very scared.

I'm still scared of being alone and often sleep with my Mum and Dad. I know my friends think I'm stupid.

We can also worry about our own safety:

Last Saturday I came back from a tour of Brisbane and Sydney and I was scared because that was the day Mum died and that is our best friend's birthday and last year Mum died on her birthday and the year before her pet died so I thought we might crash or something.

and even just 'death' itself.

Death is the one thing that I'm REALLY afraid of

Death frightens me because I haven't done enough yet.

Unfortunately death is inevitable but it is terrible to think about it. I think about it a lot.

I, myself, am afraid of death. I have heard stories that dying is peaceful and beautiful. But it still doesn't change anything.

With so much conflict going on inside us it can become difficult to cope with ordinary daily routines like going to school or work. Even going out and being with friends can seem tiresome and meaningless.

For the first month or so in class I'd just sit there and stare out the window.

I wouldn't go out anywhere, talk to my family or do anything. I'd just stay in my bedroom or I'd take my dog for a walk and sit on the beach with him for hours just thinking about what happened and how it happened. I just wanted to be by myself.

If we're feeling angry with the world and the people around us we may feel like hitting out, yelling, swearing and smashing.

Anger and frustration hit me and I broke nearly everything in my bedroom. I began to try and hurt myself by bashing my head on the wall.

When Mum told me John died I smashed my china rabbit . . . I was grumpy and said, 'Why, why, why?'

Yeah, I cried . . . it was a couple of days after. I sat in my bedroom, banging the desk a bit and let it out.

Sometimes, all we can do is cry about what's happened. And cry and cry.

I cried till it hurt.

I thought that after the tears I spilt on her grave, I couldn't cry any more. But when I think about the great adventures we had I just can't help it.

I remember crying so hard that my insides felt like coming out.

It might sound strange to say this but crying is a very healthy way of coping with our feelings. Crying helps to relieve some of the strain and the tension that has built up inside us.

Crying . . . it's a funny feeling afterwards – relief. You've gotta bawl.

The old saying 'Men shouldn't cry' - it's a whole lot of garbage. This macho thing - that's what's wrong with our society. If men could be seen to have feelings, we'd be a whole lot better off.

Crying is just one way we can help ourselves. There are other ways too.

PART II

COPING

CHAPTER 4

Handling your reactions

Talk it out . . . Talk to God.
Tell your diary.
Even your dog.

It's natural to feel helpless or overwhelmed when you're grieving. For many people it is not only a time of sadness but real confusion as well.

Sometimes I feel like I'm going crazy.

There's no denying that the road leading to the future can be very rough with jagged rocks that block our way and make us stumble. We might even think that it's too hard to keep on going.

I've been tempted to end it so I wouldn't have to cope.

I could have run for miles and I wanted to lock myself in my room and never come out.

Grief can rob us of our energy to act and cloud our vision. Remember though, inside us all we have the makings of what we need for survival. Sometimes we simply need directions to point the way and get us started.

One of the most effective ways of handling your feelings is to get them 'off your chest'. You have to find a way of releasing the feelings inside you so that they don't stay there forever. Some people say, 'Time will heal', but time alone doesn't have any magical healing powers. You have to use your time in a way that constructively allows your feelings to be expressed so that they don't stay bottled up inside you.

Here are some suggestions which could help:

TALK IT OUT

Talk to a friend, someone you trust. Talk to God. Tell your diary. Even your dog. You only need one special person who'll listen. Sometimes, just getting the words out of your mouth helps to clarify something that has been mulling around in your mind.

CREATIVELY EXPRESS YOURSELF

Sometimes you may not feel like talking about your feelings. They could be too private or perhaps you can't find the right words. Maybe, you would rather express yourself through dance or song. You can allow your movements, gestures and rhythm to identify your thoughts and feelings.

Similarly you can use art to bridge the silence when words seem empty. Through painting, drawing, clay-modelling and woodwork you can let shape, form, texture and colour be your words.

KEEP SOME MEMENTOS

Photographs, jewellery, letters, a favourite jumper or anything else that helps you to remember. You can create your own book of memories or compile a scrapbook which tells the life story of the person who has died.

Remembering can hurt in the beginning. Gradually though, this hurt lessens and is replaced by memories which can give you pleasure and comfort in the future.

EXERCISE

Playing sport, jogging, a long walk or bike ride in the fresh air can help you use up some of the nervous energy which may have built up inside you.

If you're feeling frustrated or aggressive it's better to smash a tennis ball or let fly with a golf club than it is to beat up someone in the school yard. When you're hurt or angry and life seems unfair, taking it out on others doesn't deal with the real problem. In fact, it probably just creates more.

LISTEN TO MUSIC

Music has a special way of getting through to our feelings. When we're sad we might automatically lean towards sad songs because we can identify with the words and the slow rhythm. But it's all right to listen to happy music too. This can take our minds off our sadness for a time and remind us that there is still a lot of fun out there in the world.

TAKE CARE OF YOURSELF

Grief can affect your health and your energy level. Some people feel as though they just can't be bothered and are disinterested in what's going on around them. Sometimes aches and pains, nausea and stomach upsets develop. Try to eat sensibly, even if it's only a little bit.

Also be aware of the danger of relying on alcohol or drugs to 'block out' feelings or memories. They only have an effect for a short time and you end up having to face your problems anyway.

ASK FOR HELP

This may not be so easy. It takes courage to ask for help and a certain amount of personal awareness to know when a problem has become too big to handle alone.

Ask a person whom you like and trust. It could be a relative, friend or neighbour or someone from your church. It might be a particular teacher or student counsellor.

ACCEPT YOURSELF AND YOUR REACTIONS

When you say to yourself, 'It's all right to feel the way I do', then you won't fight the normal reactions which your body is having. Then, when you allow the feelings to come out, they make way for understanding, healing and acceptance of what has happened.

> *I think drinking, drugs, violence is not facing reality . . . it's running away from it . . . Face it when it's a small problem before it becomes a big one.*

> *It was harder to talk about it than to mull over it in your head . . . You know, there's a lump in your throat.*

> *Talking about things is the best thing you can do. If you're having problems talk it out.*

> *I get angry, sad, this and that, but I keep saying it's perfectly normal, it's nothing to be ashamed of.*

> *When I go to the cemetery I tell her everything that's going on – like which guys I'm rapt in, 'cause we always used to talk about things like that.*

CHAPTER 5

Speaking out

I was thinking about Ted – how he went out in the bay to catch some snapper but never came back.

Since we can't avoid grief, we need to find some way to think about it so that it makes sense for us.

Speaking your thoughts on to paper is one way of doing this. It can clear the stuff that's muddling around in your head. You can stop and start, again and again, until you find the right words to match your feelings. Then write them down - in a letter or keep a journal. Compose a poem or song. All of these can help you say the things that you are feeling.

Maybe like:

I'm sorry.
I miss you.
I'm angry about what's happened.
I love you.
I wish I could tell you . . .
I'm glad we knew each other.
I'll always remember you because . . .

The following pages contain some examples.

GRANDMA

I never thought the day would come,
The day when she would die.
She'd always been so healthy,
Always been so well.

I couldn't believe she'd really gone
For days and weeks on end,
I'd cry myself to sleep each night
And wish her back again.

The funeral was moving
All she would have wanted.
The flowers in favourite colour
Laid down on her grave.

Now I wonder why I didn't,
Visit her more often.
And wish to take back all those things,
I said when I got cross.

My grandma was a special person,
Close to my heart,
And now I wish she was still here,
Still healthy and alive.

If only I could see her
Just one more time at least,
To tell her that I love her,
Oh how I wish I could.

The things I got, when she died
I guard with all my heart.
I keep them safely tucked away
For no one else to find.

Now when I think about the times
We had when she was here,
I still can see her smiling face
Oh what a sight it was!

I never will forget her
As long as I do live,
And hope to God that once again
I'll see her smiling face.

Wherever I may go in life,
Whatever I may do,
The memories of my grandma,
Will always be there too.

Joanne, aged 14

MY FISHING MATE

I went fishing in a boat by myself in a row boat and only caught two whiting and one leather jacket. I rowed the boat about half a kilometre out in the bay and anchored there. I was thinking about Ted - how he went out in the bay to catch some snapper but never came back - he drowned, I loved him heaps, like a second dad.

He taught me a lot about shooting rabbits and safety and fishing in the boat. He used to stay out there all night and come back in the morning. I used to stay out there heaps of times with him and Graham - his mate from work. One night I went out floundering all night with Ted. We speared forty flounder and nine big flatheads. Then we came back to the boat around about five o'clock in the morning. When I got to sleep the mossies were on patrol and I got bitten all over the cheeks. When we woke Ted said I was throwing punches everywhere and hit Ted in the ribs . . . hc said it hurt him.

The first time I went fishing with him I caught forty whiting by myself while Ted and Graham were snapper fishing. When I was in the boat sleeping, I heard them talking about me. They were saying things about my fishing. Ted was saying that for the first time, I was good. That made me very proud, coming from Ted and Graham.

When we went shooting, I was walking with

Ted. We walked around the corner and six rabbits jumped out and he only had two shots and he got two rabbits. He was eager to teach me everything he knew. I knew him about five years and he still didn't teach me everything. Ted took me snapper fishing, duck shooting and rabbit shooting but he didn't take me spotlighting - he wasn't around long enough.

I wish he was still here to teach me more things I don't know. I miss him heaps. I feel like joining him all the time. I feel like joining him now. He was the best man I have ever met before - besides my dad. I liked it when he would sit outside and talk to me about all his adventures for about two hours.

I've got heaps more to write about Ted.

Troy, aged 15

SHAUN

Your name is Shaun
and since you were born
you gave us nothing but love.
It broke my heart
when we had to part
but you're safe now in the heavens above.

We loved you for nine months
And lost you in a night
I didn't even say goodbye
You were a ray of sunshine
that lit up my life
I wish it was me
Instead of you that had to die.

It will never sink in
that your cheeky little grin
Never again will I see
Your hair was all curls
golden soft swirls
You'll always be part of me.

Lloyd, aged 14,
written in memory
of his nephew

ABOUT MY BROTHER

I felt sad and upset but then I wouldn't think about him until someone else talked about him.

I remember that he liked to kick the footy and liked to have a surf, had a lot of friends and liked lollies.

I don't like it at all that he died, but I can't really do much about it.

Adam, now 14,
writes about his brother Sam
who died when Adam was 9 years old.

MY IMAGINARY FRIEND – INGRID

I don't have a 'real' imaginary friend, but if I did have one, it would be like my best friend, Ingrid, who was killed crossing a street in March.

Ingrid was the best friend I ever had. I'm not saying I don't like my friends now, I'm just saying Ingrid fits into the best friend description perfectly. She was kind and generous and if someone was angry with her she would never fight back and call them names.

When we went overseas she said goodbye, and greeted us when we came back and if we were to come back at three in the morning, Ingrid would be there.

She was a very creative person and her writing was the prettiest I've ever seen. Ingrid could put her thoughts on to paper, like when she wrote to me she'd write something like this:

> *Dear best friend, I think you are the luckiest girl in the world to be going overseas. Make sure you bring me back some treasures to put on my desk as memoirs. Please, please write to me because as you know the postman has a thing about my name because I never get any letters. Grant my wish fairy Godmother . . . or else!*
> *Love Ingoe the dingo!*

Ingrid would write three-page letters to me and describe things as if they had happened to me.

Ingrid and I have known each other since birth and have not had one single argument. Our plans for the future were to go overseas when we were 21 and hire a campervan for the trip. We planned to go to MacRobertson's Girls School and then share a flat together. I was like a diary to her, she could confide anything with me and vice versa. We understood each other's problems and took them as our own. I am still in shock. I can't believe she is dead. And it's like no one really understands what she means to me. It's like my twin sister has left forever. It's like a jigsaw of a life and the last piece is lost. I am glad I have letters that I have received from her so I can look back at all the good times we had together. If I had an imaginary friend she would be like Ingrid.

Kate, aged 12, October 1987 -
seven months after Ingrid's death

ANDREW REMEMBERS

The night that my niece died I remember as being a time of not knowing what to do, how to react or behave, what to say and to whom. In short, it was a time of extreme confusion.

A totally unexpected event will inevitably give way to totally unexpected thoughts and behaviour. It was the first death in the family that *I* had experienced, the first one that could and would affect me. It was also the most unfair. The period between the death and the funeral and the time that ensued became a turning point . . . in many ways a new world came into being. Returning to my home, family, friends, school and life, I found that I looked deeper and harder into almost everything and everyone. So much seemed superficial and trivial. I lost contact with a good many people I called friends, but I'm glad I did. I lost a lot of interests, but once again I'm glad I did. Whatever remained of my childhood went too.

I feel, in retrospect, that a lot of growing up was done very quickly. The event triggered off numerous and subtle changes in my thoughts, my behaviour, my actions, my attitudes etc. Strange to say, but as one person in our family died, something inside me was born anew.

Andrew, aged 21, reflects on the impact of his niece's death when he was 14 years old.

PART III

ACCEPTANCE

CHAPTER 6

Facing the future

. . . but on Mother's Day, her birthday and my birthday there is always that bit missing without her.

After the initial shock and disbelief, most people begin to adjust their thoughts and lifestyle to living without the person who has died.

The time it takes it readjust varies for everyone. A couple of weeks is probably not long enough to be 'over it' and, in reality, a few years is not too long. Your family and friends, however, might become impatient for you to act like your old self again sooner than you are able.

Mum and my sisters were sympathetic for a few days but then, after a while, they got quite sick of my moping around.

My dad expected me to forget about it in a matter of two days. He was hard on me and forced me to do things and go out.

Usually there is a gradual change, from being totally overwhelmed with the loss, to experiencing a few hours, then maybe a few days and then weeks when you are not so completely preoccupied with thoughts and feelings about what's happened. This doesn't mean that you have forgotten the person who died. It just means that you are slowly remembering that life and living still have meaningful things for you to share in.

Or you can look at it this way. Even when someone is alive we don't think about them all the time and it doesn't mean that we don't love them. So, when someone has died, we don't measure how much we cared by the length of time we spend thinking of them or the amount of tears we cry over losing them.

There will, however, always be times when you are faced with reminders.

> *. . . I still get depressed especially when I hear or see anything to do with a car accident. I hate seeing smashed up cars and stuff like that. I try to ignore it because it takes me back to what I went through and who I lost.*

> *Sometimes the lump in my throat comes back, but it's not there all the time now.*

> *I still cry about it some nights in bed and I still miss her terribly when we visit Grandpa, or their house, or wear the eternity ring or other jewellery I received when she died.*

Sometimes you will be reminded when you would least expect it – when you hear some music or drive past a place that you enjoyed together.

> *I feel almost over it except sometimes it just all of a sudden gets to me.*

Other times it might be on special days like birthdays, Christmas or the anniversary of the death. Some people say that their grief often returns at times like these.

Today is four months since Grandma died. I feel that I have realized and accepted that I'll never see her again but on Mother's Day, her birthday and my birthday, there is always that bit missing without her.

Grief lasts forever . . . not all of the time . . . but on days when these people were special.

Today is two years since Mum died. I feel even more sad now that my Mum has died because it's really hard not to have a mother. There are some things that I really need to talk about just to my Mum.

I got really cut on Mother's Day.

CHAPTER 7

The end of the tunnel

You can think what a bitch life is but it's important not to use it as an excuse.

When we have lived through and survived a personal tragedy it is possible to come out of it, as the old saying goes, being 'older and wiser'. Maybe even stronger. Some people describe this by saying they have become a 'changed' person. That's okay. Grief can make us look deeply into our values, beliefs, hopes and friendships. In doing so, we establish what we really value in life – which events and relationships are important to us.

This experience can make us more aware of other people with problems. Perhaps now we'll have the courage to face a grieving friend without feeling helpless or embarassed. We can offer the same support and understanding we needed when we were down.

We might even begin to understand some things about the question 'Why?' By asking 'Why?' we let out many of our feelings and explore our beliefs. Through grief we can gradually discover that some questions in life just don't have any answers. This can be hard to accept but often grief can actually be the process by which we learn to live with the question 'Why?'

We can also learn how to cope better with the other everyday bumps and bruises which crop up in our lives.

Sure, grief knocks us around, but it is all a part of the natural protest we make at losing something we valued or someone we loved.

Therefore, if we didn't ever want to experience grief, we would have to completely cut ourselves off from close relationships and new experiences. But, then, we would never know the happiness of giving love, being loved and sharing in all that life and living can offer. For most people that would be out of the question.

It's a bit like a small toddler who is learning to walk. He has to risk the bumps and bruises of falling over if he is ever going to reach, touch and personally experience all the things in the world around him. His grazed knees and some tears are worth all the trouble when he finally walks firmly on solid ground.

Maybe all of life's promises don't come true but hurt doesn't last forever. It's important to remember there is light at the end of the tunnel. Sometimes though, we just can't see it. It's like being surrounded by a dense fog and we can't find our way through. We need courage to take the risk of living. Like the toddler, we must risk the possibility of getting hurt whenever we face the challenges of life and reach for dreams.

I know that since she died I have helped a few people talk about death and it doesn't really scare me like it used to.

It's going to take a long time for me to get over it . . . I hope I'll be better off for it – for having this experience – it's probably done me good.

You can think what a bitch life is but it's important not to use it as an excuse.

It's been a big slap in the face but it's made me take a good look at myself . . . I've gained an appreciation for other people, their feelings. I've learnt that other people have needs and wants . . . you understand other people.

I've probably learnt more through this than I ever, ever will.

PART IV

HOW TO HELP

CHAPTER 8

If you are a friend

My friends were really supportive and listened to me when I needed to talk . . .

The role of friends during a time of upheaval cannot be overstated. But the task of helping can be just as unfamiliar as the process of grieving. Don't, however, let your helplessness stop you from making an approach.

Giving support to your grieving friend does not mean you have to find magical words to take away the hurt - there simply aren't any. But if your feelings are ignored, grieving can become a lonely experience. So it takes a special kind of friend who'll share the pain and stay around long after others have forgotten.

I think school was the worst, everyone saying they're sorry and within a month they had forgotten. It made me real angry.

Then when I got back to school as I was walking up the stairs everyone in my class passed me and they all said 'Hi'. They wouldn't normally do that. They were very sympathetic. Very.

Whilst there are no qualifications needed to be a good helper, there are special qualities which will make your support more effective:

Be a good listener if your friend wants to talk. This means that you won't change the subject or criticize your friend's feelings. Your friend will feel encouraged to keep talking if you simply nod your head approvingly or say something like, 'I see what you mean' or 'It sounds like you were really scared or shocked or frustrated.'

Avoid statements like 'There are others worse off than you' or 'Come off it, it can't be that bad.' This implies that you don't accept just how difficult the loss really is. Instead, let your friend tell *you* what it feels like to be hurt. Rather than saying 'I know how you feel' (because in reality you don't) a silent hug or an arm around the shoulder will let your friend know that you care.

If your friend begins to cry, don't try to stop the tears because you feel embarrassed or awkward. Share your handkerchief and cry together if you feel like it. Boys and men especially need to know that you don't think they are a 'sissy' or a 'wimp' because they are crying. Tears are natural and normal for everyone.

Invite your friend to a movie, football game, party or whatever you used to do together. Grieving people do not always have the energy or initiative to organize an outing for themselves. However, remember they may not feel like socializing just yet - not because they're sorry for themselves, but simply because they are still feeling tense, sad or mixed up. They may even feel guilty for laughing or having fun too soon after the death.

Try not to feel discouraged if your offer of help is rejected. Some people do not know how to recognize and accept help even when it is clear to others that it would benefit them. So, be patient, be available, stay around but don't be pushy.

I have only one friend that I can share my feelings with.

Every time I mention it they just don't understand me and try to change the story.

I would feel upset and ask them if they would stop talking about it too much.

Just listen instead of asking dumb questions like 'Why are you still upset?' If they would just listen when I say I want to talk.

I'd say to others just to comfort me and feel sometimes sympathetic when I really feel crazy.

And we discussed a good thing about Grandma and I laughed and they (friends) said I should have cried instead of laughed.

My friends were really supportive and listened to me when I needed to talk to someone.

People say 'I know how you feel', but they don't really. No one knows anyone one hundred per cent I don't think. But if you can share your feelings with someone who understands, it makes it better.

CHAPTER 9

If you are a parent

I don't like to be felt sorry for, but just some signs of comfort, some hugs . . .

Talk to your child about death. It is an understandable reaction of parents to want to shield their children from the rigours of this world. But, if this protection means that questions remain unanswered and beliefs are interpreted as facts, then we have not succeeded either.

It is wise to remember that our children are receiving death education every day. Through news broadcasts, horror and action movies, books, pop songs and hearsay they are exposed to a variety of concepts depicting death and dying. We must ask whether these are realistic, helpful and truthful. If not, we need to equip ourselves with reliable information to share with our children. If you are unsure where to begin, many funeral companies now employ specially trained staff to advise families on these matters.

> *Last year our class went to a funeral parlour. Before we got there I was scared and a bit upset about going. But once we got there it was quite pleasant. The man showed us around and talked to us about death and planning a funeral. After being around I no longer felt scared and I quite enjoyed learning what I did.*

Similarly, at funerals, children need to be seen and their thoughts heard. The rituals of leave-taking, which may also include seeing the body, need to be discussed and explained. Find out your child's perception of these practices. It is usually better to ask than to presume.

My father wouldn't let me go to see her after she died. He said it would have made me cry.

I did see my grandfather at the funeral parlour. It helped me realize he was dead.

My mum and my brother had to go to the Coroner's Court but I wasn't allowed to go. They said it would be too traumatic but I couldn't have felt much worse.

At the funeral I thought everyone would have been in black but they weren't, most were in colours.

I cried a lot more than I expected but it was a beautiful funeral.

You may need to speak with your children separately to ensure they do not feel pressured to respond similarly. One teenager described her grandmother's funeral saying:

I only saw the coffin but not Grandma herself. Although I don't like to think of Grandma being dead, I would have liked to have seen her one last time . . . We had the funeral at the church which Grandma attended every Sunday with her favourite hymns, and flowers in her favourite colours and with the minister who had been very close to Grandma. I know it would have been what Grandma wanted.

Yet her sister recalled:

I didn't see Grandma at the funeral parlour and I'm glad I didn't . . . The funeral was what I expected but it was a bit worse. I would have liked the minister not to have said that Grandma had said the night before that she was going to die.

Teenagers' impressions of funerals appear as varied as their grief. Yet the value and purpose of a funeral remains constant. It is not only an occasion to farewell the dead. Its purpose is just as significant for the living - young children, teenagers and adults. By participating in the rituals of saying goodbye, we lay the necessary foundations for our grief to emerge as we confront the reality that the death has really occurred.

A friend's child died. I felt sad because it was my first funeral and he was so cute and funny. I didn't believe he died.

I didn't go to the funeral because I didn't want to believe she was gone.

Mum was going to see Nan in the coffin so my sister and I trailed behind. Nan was all dressed in white with her favourite flower in her hand. I kissed her for the last time and then went out. She was cold and hard. I remember crying so hard that my insides felt like coming out. Sitting on the wooden seats I glared at the coffin. After the funeral we went through the grieving but we knew where Nan was, in Heaven where she longed to be.

If your teenager is already facing the death of someone close, consider these suggestions:

Be ready for a vast range of possible grief reactions. Let your child know it is all right to be upset or react differently to others. There is no set 'style' of grieving. If you label tears as 'weak', nightmares as 'childish' or anger as 'bad behaviour', your child may have no outlet for expressing how he or she really feels. The only solution may be to withdraw and keep these feelings suppressed which could lead to depression, frustration and resentment. This will not help his or her grief to be resolved.

Be aware of your own sense of helplessness when

it comes to observing your child in grief. Perhaps you have already realized that you can't 'kiss it better' this time. But don't underestimate how much a hug can mean, even to your otherwise 'grown-up' teenager. A smile or other gesture of encouragement and acceptance can have the same positive effect.

Create an environment in your home that says you don't have to pretend you're coping when you're not. For teenagers it can be very helpful to know how the adults around them are really feeling. Talking openly and sharing feelings, even crying together, can be therapeutic for everyone concerned.

Answer with empathy rather than advice. It's like speaking from your heart rather than your head. Compare these responses:

Teenager:
I can't stop thinking about it. It's not fair, it's not! How can things like this happen?

Parent:
Talking like that won't help you know. But you're young, you'll get over it soon enough.

And now with empathy:

Parent:
It sounds like you're really angry about all this.

I guess your head is spinning with lots more questions too. If you want to talk about it some more . . .

Empathic responses don't claim to have answers, nor do they solve the problem. Their value lies in showing that you understand and accept the feelings you have just heard. This encourages further conversation and promotes open communication.

Recognize and respect the significance of special days. Hurt feelings might re-surface or intensify at holiday times or occasions such as Mother's/Father's Day, Christmas, Valentine's Day, birthdays and anniversaries. You could enquire how your child wishes to observe this time and if you can help in any way.

I wanted to go to the cemetery on Valentine's Day but Mum didn't have time.

I can't talk to Mum and Dad. After about three months Mum said, 'It's all over now.' She feels as if I'm over it and Dad does as well . . . I cover it all up . . . If Dad just put his arm around me occasionally saying, 'I'm here if you need me' . . .

Dad keeps to himself, he really hasn't mentioned how he has been affected by his father's death.

Mum at first cried, she doesn't take death well. She didn't talk much though . . . my other sister just laughed and said she wasn't crying because she hardly ever saw Pa anyway.

I don't like to be felt sorry for, but just some signs of comfort, some hugs . . .

My Dad had recently suffered a loss so we were in the same boat. He let me do what I wanted to and listened when I wanted to talk.

CHAPTER 10

If you are a teacher

I'm pleased that the kids wanted to do something so that Amber will always be remembered.

When attending to individual students affected by the death of a family member or friend:

Acknowledge the loss with some brief, gentle words which say you know what has happened. Let your student(s) know you'll understand if they become upset and that you are approachable should they need some advice or support.

Avoid singling out students for special attention. Even though they are bereaved, teenagers still don't want to appear different from their peers.

Attend the funeral or have the school represented through a floral tribute or other form of condolence. A personal letter to your student or a visit to the family home can be an extremely welcome sign that you care.

Be patient with bereaved students who may daydream, lack interest in their studies or fall behind with assignments. Similarly, students who become aggressive, angry or unco-operative in class may need your understanding rather than some form of punishment. The opportunity to talk out feelings or some grief counselling may be helpful.

Encourage bereaved students to support each other. It can be a great relief to discover there is someone else around who has 'been through it' too and who understands exactly what you're talking about.

Talk about death and related subjects where appropriate in the curriculum. Provide opportunities for discussion, writing, drawing, sculpture, painting and group work to explore themes like dying, grief, funerals. You need not wait until death touches the school community. Enquire about guest speakers from funeral companies, hospitals, welfare agencies and support groups whose knowledge can provide a sound basis for preventative education.

Be human and share your own fears, thoughts and feelings. When it comes to death even teachers do not have to have all the answers!

. . . one particular teacher said, 'If you feel upset or anything, feel free to just walk out and pull yourself together and then come back and if it takes all lesson don't worry. Just come back when you feel all right.' And that made me feel better just to know that people do realize that you don't get over things like that quickly.

My form teacher, Mrs M, came to the funeral and I felt very warm having her there . . .

. . . and I felt I could talk to Mrs W any time I wanted. I really like the way we have a Welfare Co-ordinator.

. . . a bit of concern or understanding could be shown to people who have been affected . . . we need to know that our teachers understand.

If a student of the school has died organize a school-based memorial service. In doing so, the student's contribution to the school is recognized as well as the grief of classmates, friends and teachers. Or you could create a memorial garden, purchase library books, sports equipment or a musical instrument. A photograph of the student, with an appropriate tribute, could be placed in the school building.

For the parents of a student who has died, it can be very comforting to know that their child's death has not been ignored by the school. Schools, which take the attitude that the death must be played down so that students are not overly upset, are falling into the trap of believing that if we ignore it, it will all go away.

There are many ways in which a school community can choose to remember:

In November 1988, Amber, a Year 6 student of a country primary school, died as a result of crime. It was decided that funds raised by her class would be used to purchase a memorial plaque which was to be affixed to a bluestone corridor within the school building.

A simple ceremony, attended by Amber's family, her closest school friends and their parents, was led by the principal on 29 May 1989, coinciding with her twelfth birthday.

I am pleased that the kids wanted to do something so that Amber will always be remembered . . . The school did other things too like the guard of honour at her funeral. And one of her teachers gave us a videotape he'd made up of all the camps Amber had attended during her years at the school. I was also told that the school band dedicated the song 'Memory' to Amber at the end of year ceremony to farewell grade 6 students . . . I think it's nice that they want to remember.

Amber's mother

When Tristan, aged ten, died through injuries he received in an accident, his teacher and classmates put together this poem which they inserted as a death notice in the local newspaper.

We will miss the jokes and whinges
We will miss the cheeky grin
We will miss the games of downball
We will miss the constant din
We will miss the confrontation
We will miss the chatter too
But most of all the thing we'll miss
Is the one and only you.

Because of the honest, yet sensitive portrait the poem created, Tristan's parents asked that it be read to commence his funeral service.

In the event of a crisis which affects the entire school - a multiple fatality, bomb threat, hostage incident or fire in the school building, a comprehensive intervention - a school recovery programme will be necessary. Such a strategy should:

Identify the person responsible for the co-ordination of the recovery programme.

Ensure means of providing accurate information about the event to staff, students and parents without delay. Rumours occur frequently when a disaster strikes and, at times, media reports are inconsistent with the actual chain of events. Swift action to dispel rumours can prevent heightened anxiety, hysteria and unrest amongst the students.

Allow students to express feelings, concerns and questions. Usual classroom lessons may need to be replaced with discussion, writing or drawing activities designed to draw out personal responses. Remember there are no right or wrong answers when we are talking about feelings so don't be tempted to assess this work with a mark out of ten! The teacher's role might simply be to identify and explain common reactions to stress and grief to normalize feelings and provide reassurance.

Aim to re-establish the school routine as soon as practicable. While the normal timetable may need to be temporarily abandoned, returning to regular activities establishes security. It indicates that the school is still in control even if the outside world seems like it's gone crazy.

Monitor behaviour and identify students at risk. Some students may be affected by this event for many months, even years. For others, past experiences of loss may surface to complicate their present reactions. Dramatic mood swings, negative themes in written work, talk of suicide, truancy, decline in work standards, apathy, violent outbursts and attention-seeking behaviour should alert teachers.

Recognize the burden of caring. Staff members, whose normal teaching duties are suddenly swamped with the additional tasks of counselling, consoling, organizing and responding, will need support too. A slap on the back accompanied by an approving 'Keep up the good work', may recognize a job well done. But do consider the impact of an arm around the shoulder and an enquiry that says, 'And how are you holding up through all this?' Designated time out to restore their energy and consider their own needs is vital if teachers are to remain effective.

CHAPTER 11

For adults only

I kind of keep it bottled up in the open but when I'm by myself I cry and think.

Normal adolescence can be a bewildering and complex developmental stage. It is a time of physical, intellectual, emotional, spiritual and sexual changes. Further complications can arise when faced with the upheaval of loss and the stress of grief. It is little wonder that so many teenagers feel misunderstood.

Even from an early age children encounter death-related situations in their daily lives. From seeing a dead animal on the road to losing a much-loved pet, children are exposed to the idea that living things die.

Around the ages of eight, nine and ten children begin to grasp the notion that death is permanent and it is universal. People die too. By the time children reach adolescence, their understanding of death is similar to that of adults. Logically then, their reactions to the death of someone close will also be as legitimate and painful as it often is for adults.

But the grief of teenagers often goes unnoticed. Maybe it's because they're young and we expect them to bounce back or forget quickly. Or perhaps it's because there is no special way of identifying a grieving teenager. When they lose a parent they are not 'widowed' or 'divorced'. Or if their best friend dies they are not considered to be primary mourners. Nor do they qualify for compassionate leave. Other forms of teenage loss may also be ignored. These include the ending of an intense relationship, abortion, changing schools, the death of a television hero or pop star, failing an exam, missing out on a job or just seeing themselves as too fat, too thin or plain and ugly.

Teenagers may also mourn the loss of childhood ideals as they search for their place amidst the demands of home, school, friends and the future. They begin to learn of the vast extremes between independence and insecurity, exuberance and disappointment, love and rejection, achievement and criticism, trust and greater responsibility.

Now add to this the challenge of understanding death and coping with the resulting feelings. Feelings like:

loneliness
depression
confusion
numbness
anger
fear
panic
rejection
guilt
sadness
anxiety
indifference

And reactions like:

aggression
poor appetite
regression
drug taking
crying
sleep disturbances
withdrawal
truancy
nervous giggling
low energy
nausea
day dreaming
denial
aches and pains

The ripple effect of grief will mean that teenagers are likely to face a number of intellectual and spiritual dilemmas as well. These may be seen as additional personal losses. Loss of:

the future - '*Things won't be the same anymore.*'
ideals - '*I thought this couldn't happen to me.*'
trust - '*Why did God let this happen?*'
security - '*It could have been me.*'
self image - '*I can't cope.*'
power - '*There's nothing I can do.*'
the will to live - '*I don't want to go on.*'
perceived support - '*No one understands me.*'

Teenagers are often unsure where to turn or how to express their innermost thoughts. They may even be further hindered by society's general expectations:

Big boys don't cry.

or those of others around them:

You're the man of the house now.

or personal pressure:

I should be over it by now.

When their feelings are not recognized or because they cannot find the words or means to express them, many adolescents simply survive by pretence.

> *When I'm around people I cover my thoughts and feelings up and they don't really know what is going through my mind. They all think that I'm over it but I'm not.*

> *I kind of keep it bottled up in the open but when I'm by myself I cry and think.*

It is important that adolescents resolve their childhood losses so that crises in their adult lives are not complicated with hurt and pain from the past. Some will choose not even to reach adulthood. Statistics will support that suicide is a significant cause of death among teenagers. This affects young people of all backgrounds who are stressed by such events as family instability, illness, death, physical disabilities, broken relationships, unfulfilled expectations and other forms of loss. Sometimes an accumulation of these events can trigger a sense of hopelessness and helplessness. Naturally there will be other complex reasons behind a decision not to live any more. When teenagers perceive themselves as isolated - when there is a belief that no one understands and no one cares - there is increased vulnerability.

So how do we communicate that we are at least trying to understand? What is the role of those who want to show they really care? A simplified answer lies in awareness and communication. For teenagers, being sensitive to the causes and effects of their griefs will lead to a better understanding of their needs. Feelings will not be trivialized. Depressive or defiant behaviour will not immediately be judged as anti-social. Self esteem will be nurtured rather than criticism and blame. To promote communication we often hear the advice that parents should talk more to their kids. But I wonder whether we shouldn't talk less and listen more! The act of listening and then responding to what we have heard with empathy is often described as 'walking in someone else's shoes'. Try walking in your teenager's sneakers, thongs or boots and you may picture the world quite differently.

This very point was made clear to me by my daughter when she was just six years old. I recall having eaten too much for dinner one evening and, sitting in front of the television, I wished I'd not had that last helping. My daughter came in saying, 'I want something else to eat. I'm hungry.' I couldn't believe it. I was so full and she was asking for more to eat! 'You can't possibly be feeling hungry,' I replied. 'Well I am,' she protested. 'Anyway, you don't feel what I feel, Mummy.'

You see, we both had a different picture. When we take the time to hear our children, growing up will seem less lonely.

IN MEMORIAM

Jenny Ryan, aged 15, died after being involved in a road accident. Some of her friends have contributed to the writing of this book.

Jenny was a spirited girl. She was an independent thinker, who often wrote poetry to express her inner thoughts. It was her ambition to become a journalist and to have her work published.

Jenny did not live to fulfil this dream in her lifetime. By including one of her poems in this book, written in memory of her own father, we can share in Jenny's dream and perpetuate her memory.

It was the year 1977, the first day of September,
For this is the day I'll always remember,
The year the day I will never forget,
and look upon it with sad regret,
For this is the day my father died,
It wasn't till years later that I cried,
And when he died I was only five,
I didn't understand the word survive,
Survive he didn't . . . die he did,
And when he died I was only a kid,
Dead at thirty-eight years of age,
My heart broke with anger and rage,
Why did he die, why was it so?
No one could tell me, they didn't know,
They said: 'The good die young . . . The bad live on.'
If he was bad he wouldn't have gone,
Ten years later and yet I still cry,
I didn't get a chance to say good-bye,
But in my mind you live on,
My love for you is an everlasting bond,
Although you were sick for many a year,
Not once did you show me your dying fear,
Even though you're gone to a different place,
Never in my life shall I forget your face.

Jennifer Anne Ryan
27 July 1972–2 March 1988

SUGGESTED READING

Books suitable for teenagers:

FICTION:

Day, David, *Are You Listening Karen?* Puffin Books, 1983.

Paterson, Katherine, *Bridge to Terebithia*, Puffin Books, 1972.

Pershall, Mary K., *You Take the High Road*, Penguin Books, 1988.

NON FICTION:

Krementz, Jill, *How It Feels When a Parent Dies*, Alfred A. Knopf, 1982.

LeShan, Eda, *Learning To Say Goodbye*, Macmillan, 1976.

BOOKS FOR ADULT READERS:

Bennett, Dr David, *Growing Pains - What To Do When Your Children Turn Into Teenagers*, Doubleday Australia, 1987.

Fabian, Suzanne, *The Last Taboo*, Penguin, 1986.

Grollman, Earl A. (ed.), *Talking About Death - A Dialogue Between Parent and Child*, Beacon Press, 1970.

Kubler-Ross, Elizabeth, *On Children and Death*, Macmillan, 1983.

McKissock, Mal, *Coping With Grief*, A.B.C. Enterprises, 1985.

Staudacher, Carol, *Beyond Grief*, New Harbinger Publications Inc., 1987.

Westberg, Granger, *Good Grief*, Joint Board of Christian Education, 1985.

SPECIALIST BOOKS FOR TEACHERS AND COUNSELLORS

Raphael, Beverley, *The Anatomy of Bereavement*, Hutchinson, 1984.

Rosen, Helen, *Unspoken Grief - Coping With Childhood Sibling Loss*, Lexington Books, 1986.

Wolfelt, Alan, *Helping Children Cope With Grief*, Accelerated Development Inc., 1988.

Worden, J. William, *Grief Counselling and Grief Therapy*, Springer Publishing Co., 1982.